Bigger, Better, Stronger!

Contents

Written by Rob Alcraft

Illustrated by Alan Rowe

Collins

Meet the contenders

Are you stronger than an ant?
Are you a better jumper than a frog?

What if you were no bigger than them?

Ant

Some ants can pick up **loads** that are like lifting 100 ants.

To win, you must lift six cows.

The ant is stronger!

Tree frog

A tree frog can jump as far as 44 tree frogs.

To win, you must **clear** 15 cars.

The tree frog
jumps further!

Shark

A shark swims at killer speed.

You need a speed boat to **secure** a win.

The shark is quicker!

Froghopper

A froghopper is an **expert** high jumper.

To win, you must jump higher than
a tower block.

The froghopper
jumps higher!

Falcon

A falcon **stars** at high speed flight.

pure speed

To zoom quicker in the air you need a rocket.

The falcon is quicker!

13

Black mamba

Black mambas are astonishing **sprinters**!

A mamba has no legs but is quicker than you in short sprints.

The mamba is quicker!

Mantis

A mantis is a star hunter.

lightning speed

A mantis grabs quicker than you can blink.

You!

Lots of animals are quicker and stronger than you – and better jumpers.

But do not **despair**.
You claim the bigger brain!

Glossary

clear jump further than

despair feel bad

expert An expert has a lot of skills.

loads things to lift

secure When you secure a thing, you gain or get it.

sprinters runners

stars performs well

Index

Winners!

best lifter

best jumpers

After reading

Letters and Sounds: Phases 3 and 4

Word count: 215

Focus phonemes: /sh/ /th/ /ng/ /ai/ /ee/ /igh/ /oa/ /oo/ /ar/ /ur/ /ow/ /ear/ /air/ /ure/ /er/, and adjacent consonants

Common exception words: of, to, the, no, are, you, like, were, when, what, some, do

Curriculum links: Science: Animals, including humans

National Curriculum learning objectives: Reading/word reading: read accurately by blending sounds in unfamiliar words containing GPCs that have been taught; read other words of more than one syllable that contain taught GPCs; read words containing taught GPCs and –s, –es, –ing, –ed, –er and –est endings; Reading/comprehension (KS2): understand what they read, in books they can read independently, by checking that the text makes sense to them, discussing their understanding and explaining the meaning of words in context; identifying main ideas drawn from more than one paragraph and summarising these

Developing fluency

- Take turns to read a page, demonstrating how to alter your tone for sentences ending in question marks and exclamation marks.
- Check your child remembers to pause at full stops, and to very briefly pause at commas and at the dash on page 18.

Phonic practice

- Practise reading words with more than one syllable, breaking them up into syllables:

  con-ten-ders   jump-er   ex-pert   sprint-ers   ast-on-ish-ing

- Take turns to find and read a word ending in –er or –ers.

Extending vocabulary

- Ask your child which of the following words they can add –er or –ing to the end to make a new word:

  high   pick   fair   rocket   speed   tower   blink

- Discuss the meanings of the new words and challenge your child to put one into a sentence.